MW01156331

Because of
JESUS

Because of
Jesus

Because of JESUS

Kenneth Hagin Jr.

Unless otherwise indicated, all Scripture quotations in this volume are from the *King James Version* of the Bible.

Second Edition
Seventh Printing 1998

ISBN 0-89276-701-4

In the U.S. write:
Kenneth Hagin Ministries
P.O. Box 50126
Tulsa, OK 74150-0126

In Canada write:
Kenneth Hagin Ministries
P.O. Box 335, Station D
Etobicoke (Toronto), Ontario
Canada, M9A 4X3

Copyright © 1986 RHEMA Bible Church
AKA Kenneth Hagin Ministries, Inc.
All Rights Reserved
Printed in USA

The Faith Shield is a trademark of RHEMA Bible Church, AKA Kenneth Hagin Ministries, Inc., registered with the U.S. Patent and Trademark Office and therefore may not be duplicated.

Contents

1. He Is the Christ 1

2. Because of Jesus 23

3. Jesus Christ Cures You 45

Chapter 1

He Is the Christ

When Jesus came into the coasts of Caesarea Philippi, he asked his disciples, saying, Whom do men say that I the Son of man am?

And they said, Some say that thou art John the Baptist; some, Elias; and others, Jeremias, or one of the prophets.

He saith unto them, But whom say ye that I am?

And Simon Peter answered and said, Thou art the Christ, the Son of the living God.

— Matthew 16:13-16

In this day and age, people are still splitting theological hairs over the question: "Who is Jesus?"

Some say, "He was a great this. He was a great that. He was a mere man. He wasn't a mere man. He was a great teacher. He was a great *prophet*. He was the greatest moral person who ever lived."

Jesus was the greatest teacher the world has ever known. He was the greatest preacher the world has ever heard. But He is more than all of this.

Jesus is the Husband to the bride.

He is the Friend to the friendless.

He is the Physician to the sick.

He is the Psychiatrist to the confused.

He is the Banker to the poor.

He is the Compass to the traveler.

He is the Bright and Morning Star to the one walking in darkness.

He is the Healer of all sickness.

He is the Savior from every sin.

He is the Deliverer from every habit.

He is the Baptizer in the Holy Spirit and fire to everyone who hungers and thirsts.

He is the One of whom the prophet Isaiah said, " . . . *his name shall be called Wonderful, Counselor, The mighty God, The everlasting Father, The Prince of Peace*" (Isa. 9:6).

He is the Lion of the Tribe of Judah.

He is the Lily of the Valley.

He is the Alpha and the Omega.

He is the Beginning and the End.

He is the One who was. He is the One who is. He is the One who is coming again.

He is the One whom Herod could not destroy.

He is the One whom the devil could not entice into sin.

He is the One whom the grave could not hold.

He is the One who arose from the dead.

He is the Victor.

He is the One whom God has highly exalted and given a Name above every name — the Name of Jesus Christ of Nazareth.

He is the One who turned the water into wine.

He is the One who walked on the Sea of Galilee.

He is the One who spoke and the blind could see, the lame

could walk, the deaf could hear, and the mute could speak.

He is the Christ, the Son of the living God!

If I had a thousand tongues and a thousand lives, I could never tell all that Christ is. As the Apostle John said on one occasion, *". . . there are also many other things which Jesus did, the which, if they should be written every one, I suppose that even the world itself could not contain the books that should be written . . ."* (John 21:25).

You ask me, "Who is Jesus?" I have given a few answers from the Scriptures. If I were to take more time, I could extol who He is on page after page. I have simply picked out some of the most common scriptures for this lesson, starting in the beginning of the Bible and continuing all the way through to the end.

When we get to the Book of Revelation, we see Jesus riding a white horse. Across Jesus' vesture His Name is written: " . . . *KING OF KINGS, AND LORD OF LORDS*" (Rev. 19:16). I like that one!

I want you to notice Jesus became all of this because of what He did at the Cross of Calvary, because of the work of redemption that He wrought for mankind. God is still the same miracle-working God, and because of what Jesus did, we have the same power available to us today that was available to Jesus when He walked on the earth.

To understand what Jesus accomplished for us, let us now imagine a garden outside the city of Jerusalem.

I can just see the Lord with His disciples, who had been with Him throughout His ministry.

He has just finished ministering to them.

I see Him now as He enters the garden, taking Peter, James, and John with Him and leaving the other disciples behind.

He says to these three beloved disciples, "Would you pray with Me?" Then He goes a little farther into the garden alone. I see Him as He finds a place, drops upon His knees, and begins to pray to the Father.

His heart is heavy. Tears start coming from His eyes. Perspiration appears on His brow — and it is as great drops of blood (Luke 22:44).

The time has come. The sins of men — all the sins of all the men who had ever lived and who would ever live — are going to be placed upon His shoulders.

He looks toward Heaven and says, "Father, if it be possible, let this cup pass from me." What cup? The cup of bitterness — the cup of sin for all of us. This cup includes not only sin; it includes sickness. It includes all that came to mankind as the result of Adam's fall.

Here is Jesus, the Son of God, stepping out of the role He has ministered in for three years: the Son of Man anointed by the Holy Spirit. And that is exactly what He was. People say, "He did all those miracles because He was Deity." No, He did not. It was because He was anointed with the Holy Spirit that He was able to do all the miraculous things He did (Acts 10:30; Phil. 2:5-8).

But now, as the sins of the world are about to be placed upon Him, He is stepping out of that place as the Son of Man and is becoming the Lamb of God.

I see Him as He stands up in the garden where He had been

praying and returns to His disciples. He is waiting for the armed mob to come and arrest Him. They come.

I see Him as He stands in that judgment hall and they begin to mock Him. They ask Him questions. He says not a word. They ask Him, "Are You the King of the Jews?" He says, "You have said it." He answers in neither the affirmative nor the negative. He simply says, "You have stated it."

Pontius Pilate decides that there is nothing wrong with this man named Jesus. In fact, the Bible infers that Pilate is touched by the good in Jesus and perhaps wonders if He *is* the Son of God.

Pilate says to himself, *I know how I can get them to turn this man loose. It is a custom to release a prisoner at the Passover. I will offer to release either Jesus or the most horrible criminal in their nation.* He gives the mob the choice. But they accept the notorious criminal Barabbas! "Release Barabbas and crucify Jesus!" the mob screams.

Not all of the people in that riotous mob are against Jesus, however. Many are neutral. The same thing can happen today. A group of people can infest a crowd and incite them to riot. Even bystanders become caught up in the emotion and take part in the riot. No doubt, there were many people like that in this crowd.

I can envision Jesus as He stands there. They bring out a purple robe, which represents royalty, and they throw it around Him. "Hey, He needs a crown!" someone yells. The soldiers weave thorns into a crude crown and slam it down Jesus' head. I can see the blood begin to trickle down His face.

Jesus stands there. I see Him as they begin to pluck the beard from His face. Blood begins to appear in those pores. Someone walks up to Him and says, "You think You are the Son of God, huh?" and slaps Him across the face. He says not a word. He just stands there.

I go back to Isaiah 52 and 53 and begin to read. The Bible talks about Jesus' face being marred almost beyond recognition (Isa. 52:14).

I can just see Jesus as the soldiers take Him into the lower part of the fortress. I see them strip the garments off His back and lay them aside. I see them take the leather thongs and tie Him with His back exposed.

I see a Roman soldier — a big, strong, robust fellow with huge shoulder and arm muscles. I see him reach out and grab that big whip. At the end of each strand of leather in that whip is a round lead ball about the size of a quarter. Inside it is crushed glass. This is the kind of whip the Romans traditionally used.

I see Jesus as the whip begins to slash across His back. The soldier gives it a jerk so one of the balls with the crushed glass will come raking across the skin. Not only is the leather thong breaking the skin, but Jesus' back is being ripped open by crushed glass.

I see His back begin to bleed. Blood begins to splatter all over the soldier — the precious blood of God's Son Jesus Christ! Blood that could save him! Blood that could cleanse him! And he doesn't even realize it!

The soldier does not realize that the stripes he has put on Jesus' back are stripes for the healing of mankind. Some theologians say there were thirty-nine stripes to represent the thirty-nine principal causes of disease.

The Bible says, *"Who his own self bare our sins in his own body on the tree . . . by whose stripes YE WERE HEALED"* (1 Peter 2:24). Salvation and healing go hand in hand, and we see this truth in this verse of Scripture. Also, I have seen many persons healed whom we would consider rank sinners. But I have never seen them remain sinners very long after the power of God healed them. Why? Because they knew what their condition was, and they knew who healed them. They knew it wasn't medical science; it was the power of God.

Yes, with Jesus' stripes, your cancer died. Your asthma died. Your rheumatism and arthritis died.

Because of who Jesus is, every problem must bow its knee.

Because of who Jesus is, crooked legs can be straightened.

Arms and legs can grow out because of who Jesus is.

We don't have to worry about anything. We don't have to worry about demons or demonic power.

The Word of God says that when Jesus Christ died on the Cross, He did combat with Satan and defeated him. Because we are in Christ, we have the victory that Christ won for us. That is what the Word says.

Jesus is the mighty Conqueror, the mighty Deliverer, the One who can transform lives.

Yes, Jesus is the Deliverer to the one bound by alcohol, dope, or any kind of habit.

Many of you have vowed and vowed and vowed that you were going to quit smoking, quit drinking, quit taking dope, quit doing this, or quit doing that, but you never have been able to. With Jesus you can be delivered from sinful habits.

Who is Jesus? Our minds are so small that we can only see a small picture of who Jesus really is. Jesus is so powerful that our finite minds cannot even begin to understand Him.

It is because of Jesus and who Jesus is, for example, that we have the Holy Spirit and the gifts of the Spirit. Jesus, who is now sitting at the right hand of the Father, sent us the Holy Spirit with all of His gifts. It is because of Jesus that the gifts of the Spirit operate.

The Holy Spirit is real. And the Holy Spirit has come with all of His gifts and His attributes because of who Jesus is.

The Spirit of God moves as He wills (1 Cor. 12:11). We do not make Him move by going through any kind of contortions or by following any kind of set pattern. God does not move that way. The Word of God tells us that He moves *when* He chooses, *where* He chooses, and *how* He chooses.

I have seen the power of God demonstrated. I have seen miracle after miracle. I have watched a man of God walk off the platform, reach down and grab the hand of someone on a stretcher, and say, "In the Name of Jesus, rise and walk!" I have seen those who were crippled, rise and begin to run up and down the aisle. I have seen a man of God walk over to someone in a wheelchair and say, "In the Name of Jesus, walk!" And then the preacher sat down in the wheelchair himself as the former invalid pushed the preacher in the wheelchair around the church.

I have seen blind eyes snap open. I have seen deaf ears pop open. It is all because of Jesus — because of what He did and what He purchased for us at Calvary.

The Word of God says, *". . . If thou canst believe, all things are possible to him that believeth"* (Mark 9:23).

At the mighty Name of Jesus, all knees shall bow.

Because of the mighty Name of Jesus, we can receive anything that the Word promises we can receive from Him. All things are ours because of who Jesus is (1 Cor. 3:21).

He is our Victor. And because of Jesus, we have victory over sin, disease, and any other thing that would hinder us from living the God-kind of life.

The Spirit of God will manifest Himself through us if we will put Jesus in the right perspective and let Him rule in our midst. If we will get flesh and programs out of the way and just lift up Jesus, we will see something happen. It is not your program that is going to win people anyway. It is Jesus. It is not your preaching necessarily that is going to win the people. It is Jesus.

The reason we are not seeing people saved in many churches is because Jesus is not really being lifted up. The churches are doing a good job of teaching. They are doing a good job of preaching. And everyone is telling the preacher how great he is.

I appreciate compliments as much as anyone, and I say, "Thank you," but I also say, "Give the glory to Jesus." I never want to be caught taking any glory for myself.

And it is not just the preacher who faces this temptation. It also reaches down into the pew. A person who is an effective soul-winner may begin to think, *Man, look what I can do!*

Or the bus captain, for example, may begin to look at all the people on his bus and think, *Look what I've done!*

I want to tell you something: If the Holy Spirit had not moved upon those people's hearts, when you knocked on their door, they might have slammed them in your face! Do not get the mistaken idea that those people are coming to church just because you went out there knocking on doors. It is because of who Jesus is!

Let's get it in the right perspective. Let's look up to Jesus and say, "You are the Christ, the Son of the Living God!" That's what Peter said to Him. And Jesus said that was not revealed to Peter through flesh and blood, but by the Spirit of God (Matt. 16:16,17).

You and I are supposed to be Spirit-filled, on-fire people for God. Yet half of us are limited when we tell anyone who Jesus really is. We have been more concerned about everything else than about who Jesus is.

If I read the New Testament correctly, every writer, including the Apostle Paul, was concerned with telling people who Jesus is and who we as children of God are *in Him*. I know there is a lot of other information in there, too, but take the skills you learned in your English class and find out what the main theme is.

The main theme is Jesus and what He did. And when we grasp this idea of who Jesus really is, it will change our world, for we are going to change the world we live in.

The Apostle Paul said, *". . . forgetting those things which are behind . . ."* (Phil. 3:13). Paul had more good things than bad to forget, yet he included all of his accomplishments and all the other things that had happened to him before he found Christ. He said, "I don't look behind me. I set my eyes on the goal that is in front of me. I look forward to the prize of the high calling of God in Christ Jesus."

Paul set that goal, and he went forward to do something for God. That is where we go from here. We do not holler about what we received from God last month, last week, or even last night. We go forward every day with Jesus. We cannot rest on what happened yesterday or we will become stagnant Christians. The Spirit of God wants us to go forward.

Telling people about who Jesus is is the only thing that ultimately matters. When you begin to tell people about who

Jesus is, their deliverance comes, their salvation comes, their healing comes, and their prosperity comes. It all comes because of who Jesus is.

If you will forget about your big dissertations and your big theological arguments and just begin to talk about who Jesus is; if you will quit worrying about whether you are able to teach from a Sunday school quarterly and instead, get down on your face before God and say, "God, I've got the responsibility, and I want to tell people who Jesus is," then you will begin to find your place in the Body of Christ. You will begin to move forward for God.

You will find that not only are you moving forward spiritually and doing something for God, but people are being saved, blessed, and helped on every hand.

Chapter 2

Because of Jesus

Colossians 1:12 says, *"Giving thanks unto the Father, which hath made us meet to be partakers of the inheritance of the saints in light."* Partakers of what? Of the inheritance.

As children of God, we have an inheritance that includes all the provisions God made for us through all the covenants He established in His Word.

Because our inheritance is found in the New Testament, or New Covenant, we Christians should carefully study these scriptures, paying particular attention to the epistles, the letters written to the Church.

Many say, "We need to study the Book of Acts and be like the Early Church." Yes, certainly we need the power of the Holy Spirit the Early Church had, but we do not need any of the mechanics that made the Early Church operate, because believers then lived under far different circumstances than we do today.

Too many Christians skim through a Psalm or a few Proverbs and call that their daily Bible study. Then they run out and try to face the world on the strength of those few verses! Other Christians want to read only the four Gospels. We need to enjoy and study the entire Bible, but the epistles have been specifically written for believers who are living under the New Covenant.

When someone picks up your Bible, he should be able to tell at a glance where in your Bible you read the most. If you were to pick up one of my old study Bibles, you would see the worn pages where I have turned many times to the Pauline epistles. They are where I live, so to speak. They are where I read. I happen to like the man Paul. He wrote more than half of the New Testament and more epistles than anyone else.

In the epistles, we learn exactly how the Church should be operating, how believers should be living, who believers are, and what belongs to them in Christ. This is the message of the epistles.

The epistles are where our strength comes from. They are where our power comes from — the power of knowing what belongs to us *because of Jesus*.

If we do not know what belongs to us, our voice will lack authority, and we will hesitate when we begin to talk about our rights and privileges because of Jesus. And when this happens, we are not going to convince anyone, including Satan, that we have any power or authority. There are too many Christians in this predicament: They are often mouthing words that do not have any power behind them.

When I was in school in Texas, many young fellows were running around mouthing a lot of words. They bragged about who they were, what they could do, and so forth. But do you know what? There wasn't any power behind their talk. In other words, they couldn't produce results.

They could "talk" a good fight. They could "talk" a good football game. Man, they could talk about scoring more touchdowns than anyone in the country! But if you were to place the football in their hands and put them in an actual game, they would run in the wrong direction when they faced their opponent!

The same holds true of many Christians. If we do a lot of talking without knowing what is really going on, we are not going to go far when we are holding the ball and facing Satan. We might even run away from him in fear. But that shouldn't be.

Therefore, we need to go through the epistles and find out what belongs to us as Christians *because of Jesus*. There are approximately 140 key phrases in the New Testament that describe our inheritance. They tell us who we are, what we are, or what we have *because of Jesus*.

We need to underline these scriptures in red. Then we need to list all the scriptures having such phrases as "in Christ," "in Him," "in whom," "through whom," and so forth.

(If you don't want to dig out all of these scriptures yourself, my father, Rev. Kenneth E. Hagin, has put many of them into a minibook entitled, *In Him*.)

We would have nothing if it were not for Jesus — no salvation, no hope. Just a mess that would end in a holocaust — that's all there would be in the world if there were no Jesus!

But *because of Jesus*, there is hope, there is reality, there is power, there is strength, there is victory — all the time.

And as we study these scriptures about who we are and what we have *because of Jesus*, we need to *believe* them in our heart and *confess* them with our mouth daily. Confessions from God's Word of who we are in Christ make us *what we confess*.

When we begin to make a confession of God's Word — when we speak it with our mouth — it becomes *rhema*. (In the Greek, "rhema" is the *spoken* Word of God and "logos" is the *written* Word of God.)

As the Word of God comes out of our mouth, faith is created in our inner man, and we receive the power and authority to march forth as conquerors. As we speak forth the Word of God, the *rhema* Word of God becomes a weapon that destroys the works of the enemy, Satan, in our lives.

We always want to know what the perfect will of God is for us. God's perfect will for His children is that we enjoy *all* of the realities, benefits, and blessings of our inheritance as set forth in the Word of God. *That* is His perfect will.

Too many Christians, however, never have realized *all* of our inheritance belongs to us *now*. There are those who preach and teach, "We are going to get the inheritance after a while if we can get in the right place with God. In the by-and-by it's going to be sweet."

I'll tell you, it's not only going to be sweet in the by-and-by — it's sweet *right now*. It's not out there somewhere in the future. If you are a child of God — if you are in Christ — it's yours *now*.

The Word of God says that we are heirs "and joint-heirs with Christ" (Rom. 8:17). An *heir* is someone who has inherited something — it is his at the moment. If he must wait for his inheritance, he is called an *heir apparent*. But the Bible calls us *heirs*.

What did we receive? We received the inheritance of God in Christ Jesus. Let's make it alive in us. Let's put it to work for us.

If you have received the inheritance, you don't need to be sick.

If you have received the inheritance, you don't need to be sitting around in poverty.

Why don't you get up, claim what is yours in Christ Jesus, and march forward as a victor?

Some people who were invited to attend a Christian conference turned their back on their inheritance when they said, "We know the Word of God is true, but we can't afford to go. You go ahead, but we can't afford to go along with you. Maybe in a few years we'll have a nest egg and can afford to do things like that." With their mouths, they spoke the possibility of making such a trip out of existence.

Yes, you can turn your back on your inheritance. I remember reading a story about a college boy who had inherited $1 million. He refused his inheritance. He was found living in terrible poverty — yet $1 million that belonged to him was available to him in a New York City bank! The bank even sent him blank checks with which to withdraw some of his inheritance.

Sometimes we Christians are like that college boy. We live in spiritual and material poverty even though Jesus Christ has deposited all the inheritance of Heaven into our account, and we can draw from that inheritance all we want to!

The way we cash the "check" is with our mouth. (Since I discovered that, I have been cashing those kinds of "checks," and I intend to keep on cashing them!)

There are a lot of people — bless their hearts, I can't understand them — who say, "That's all right for you. You can live that way, but I can't." They are acting out the words of that old unbelieving song that says in effect, "The Lord knows I can't live on that big, large mountaintop. Just pick me out a valley."

Brother, you can live in a valley if you want to, but as for me and my house, we're going to live on the mountaintop and shout the victory!

You can live down there in the shadows if you want to, but we're going to live in the sunshine of the glory upon the mountaintop *because of Jesus*.

People say, "Praise God, fifteen people got saved last night." No, fifteen people didn't get saved last night; fifteen people just found out about their inheritance and drew from their bank account last night. That bank account was established for them some two thousand years ago when Jesus Christ died and rose again, and they just found out about it.

Have you ever heard people testifying, "Oh, I got healed last night?" No, they really didn't. They just found out about it, wrote a "check," and cashed it, so to speak, by believing and acting on it.

Healing was established for us when Jesus took the stripes on His back. That's what the Word says. *Because of Jesus*, healing belongs to us.

There is a principle involved in knowing what we have *because of Jesus*. It is this: *If we have scriptures to back what we are speaking with our mouth, we will create the reality of it in our lives the way God creates realities when He speaks.*

In other words, when we speak in line with the Word of God, we create something — we bring something into being with the confession of our mouth.

But it never will happen until we speak it with our mouth. We can *think* it in our mind. We can *know* it in our heart. But until we *speak* it with our mouth, it never will happen! That is cashing the check. *Writing* checks all day long will never do us any good until we go out and *cash* them.

"For with the heart man believeth unto righteousness; and WITH THE MOUTH CONFESSION IS MADE UNTO SALVATION" (Rom. 10:10). The very foundation for our confession of faith is Jesus and what He accomplished.

Always remember: It is because of the foundation Christ established that our confession is made. It is *because of Jesus* that we have an inheritance. It is nothing we ourselves have done.

Faith is real, and faith's confessions will create realities because we are *in Christ*.

Unfortunately, many people begin to get full of pride after

they find the secret of success with God.

If they begin to say, "I'm spiritual. I've got more faith than anyone," they might as well quit trying to cash the "checks" because it isn't going to work. They have their values misplaced. They are saying, "Look at what *I* can do. Man, I can speak it, and it will come into existence." They are forgetting about Jesus Christ. It is *because of Jesus* that faith and prayer work!

We find an Old Testament example of this in the life of Saul. Everything was fine when Saul first became king of Israel. Then King Saul suddenly began to lose his humble spirit — his meekness before God. He tucked his thumbs in his vest, so to speak, and said, "Look at who I am. I'm the *king!*" His road was downhill from then on.

Anyone who thinks he has become so strong in faith that he can say, "Look at me! Look at my faith!" in a proud, boastful manner is in for a big fall.

The 140 faith confession scriptures may not seem real to you as you begin to read and confess them, but if you keep on confessing them even if you have to confess them to yourself in your mirror — you will start believing them eventually.

Confess them because they are the Word of God. Then you will start believing them with your heart. And when you start believing them in your heart, things will start happening because you are confessing the Word with your mouth.

The believing and the confessing will create the realities in your life.

Let us look at another scripture: *"Blessed be the God and*

Father of our Lord Jesus Christ, who hath blessed us with all spiritual blessings in heavenly places in Christ" (Eph. 1:3).

That scripture doesn't say, "Blessed be the God and Father of our Lord Jesus Christ, who will give us blessings when we comb our hair right and look right . . . ." That scripture does not say I have to wear a coat when I preach, does it? It does not say I have to comb my hair a certain way to get a blessing, does it? No, it doesn't say any of those things.

It says, *"Blessed be the God and Father of our Lord Jesus Christ, who HATH BLESSED US with all spiritual blessings in heavenly places in Christ."*

There is nothing in this scripture that says God *is going to do* something. There is nothing that says God will do something if we line up with a certain set of rules and regulations or if we do this, that, or the other.

No, He *has already done it* because we are in Christ. He *has already blessed us* because we are *in Him*.

This means that from the time we became a born-again Christian until the time we step out into eternity, all spiritual blessings are ours — *whether we use them or not!* They already are credited to our account. God has blessed us with everything we need. We need not want for anything. We need not be concerned for anything. He already has blessed us with all things pertaining to life and godliness (2 Peter 1:3).

All we need to do is find out what belongs to us — what our inheritance really is — begin to confess it, act like it is so, and *make it become a reality*.

Someone might say, "But you don't understand . . . ."

That's right. I don't understand. That is, I don't understand someone who has gone to school and has learned to read, yet does not understand the English language. The diploma hanging on his wall says he is a graduate, yet he doesn't understand the simple Word of God which says, "If you believe it and receive it, it belongs to you."

Healing belongs to us. It is part of our inheritance. Financial blessing belongs to us. That also is part of our inheritance. Those are the two areas we are most concerned about in this life!

There is much more that belongs to us that you need to discover from reading God's Word. No minister can give it all to you at one time. All I can do is try to give you something you can believe, put into action, and begin to study for yourself with the Holy Spirit as your Teacher.

Study the realities of God. Don't let them lie dormant. When they lie dormant, your life becomes like a stagnant pool of water. Why? Because nothing is flowing into it and nothing is flowing out of it. That is exactly what happens to many Christians. They shut off the channel of blessing because their faith is dormant or inactive.

In the mind of God, He already has given us everything we need in this life. It is up to us to possess it! Let us begin to live at the level at which our Father intended us to live.

Even earthly fathers want their children to enjoy the same social and economic status they enjoy or *better*. Likewise, our Heavenly Father wants us to live on the best level that we can in every area of our lives. So we need to appropriate by faith what belongs to us.

God wants us to live at this level of victory with every need met, every victory won, walking through life like a child of the King, carefree and happy. Hallelujah, that is exactly the way we should be. We should be marching through life as kings and queens. The Word of God belongs to us.

Have you ever seen a king walking around with his head down, muttering, "Boy, I sure would like to have a new car like that"?

No! A king would say, "Go get me a car. Go get me this. Go get me that." A king has people who work for him.

I want to tell you something. You and I as children of God have someone to work for us too. Angels, ministering spirits of God, work for us! Hebrews 1:14

says, *"Are they not all ministering spirits, sent forth to minister for them who shall be heirs of salvation?"* All we have to do is begin to command the angels to minister for us according to God's Word.

We are kings! Because we are in Jesus Christ, we are kings! The Word of God says that we will rule with Him: ". . . those who receive [God's] overflowing grace (unmerited favor) and the free gift of righteousness [putting them into right standing with Himself] reign as kings in life through the one Man, Jesus Christ (the Messiah, the Anointed One)" (Rom. 5:17 *Amp.*).

The Word of God calls Jesus Christ the King of kings. If I'm in Christ, and I'm ruling with Him, then I'm a king, too, and I'm going to start acting like it.

Let's start acting like we're kings!

Let's start living like we're kings!

Let's start claiming what is ours!

Kings sweep the garbage out of the back door of their palaces. That is what we need to do with Satan. We can't keep him from coming around, but we certainly can keep him from *staying* around!

We are to live by the Word of God, confess the Word of God, and watch it become a reality in our lives. We are to live the life of a victor. The victory is ours.

I'm going to Heaven shouting the victory! Nothing is going to bother me or cause me to be downcast and defeated. I challenge you to live the victorious life *because of Jesus.*

Chapter 3

Jesus Christ Cures You

And it came to pass, as Peter passed throughout all quarters, he came down also to the saints which dwelt at Lydda.

And there he found a certain man named Aeneas, which had kept his bed eight years, and was sick of the palsy.

And Peter said unto him, Aeneas, Jesus Christ maketh thee whole: arise, and make thy bed. And he arose immediately.

And all that dwelt at Lydda and Saron saw him, and turned to the Lord.

— Acts 9:32-35

This portion of Scripture tells the story of a helpless paralytic named Aeneas, who was healed when Peter told him, ". . . Aeneas, Jesus Christ cures you . . ." (Acts 9:34 *Weymouth*).

As the story opens, we see a man named Peter who has been scurrying from town to town, village to village, synagogue to synagogue, and anywhere else he could preach.

Peter is telling the people about Jesus Christ, the Man with whom he walked; the Man whom he saw die on the Cross for them; the Man whom he saw ascend from the Mount of Olives on a cloud of glory after telling His disciples, ". . . *tarry ye in the city of Jerusalem, until ye be endued with power from on high*" (Luke 24:49).

And now Peter has come to Lydda. Can't you see him as he finishes his first service and one of the brethren runs up to him and says, "Oh, Peter, we've got a sad case here — a man by the name of Aeneas. He has been paralyzed for eight years. Will you go see him? He can't make it out to the services."

In my mind's eye, I go down to Aeneas' house with Peter. I see Peter approach Aeneas' sickbed, and I see Aeneas look up sadly.

He asks Peter, "What are you doing here? I've tried all the doctors. I've done everything I know to do, and I'm still not any better. They say it's incurable. What kind of a new idea do *you* have?

I see a smile break across Peter's face. I know immediately that his mind is racing back to a certain day just after the Holy Spirit had been poured out — a day recounted in the third chapter of Acts.

In his memory, Peter walks up once again to the Gate called

Beautiful. A wretched beggar sits beside the gate. He stinks with the stench of all the animals and people who have been walking by kicking dust and dirt on him.

There he sits, shaking that little tin cup, rattling those coins in the bottom of it as if to say, "Give me some money!'

I see Peter as he walks up to that beggar and says, "I don't have any silver, and I don't have any gold. But such as I have, give I you!" (Acts 3:1-8).

Peter saw that beggar leap and walk that day, healed by the power of God. And as he looks down at Aeneas, he says, "Aeneas, I can help you!"

I am sure Peter also told Aeneas, "Now, Aeneas, Jesus Christ is the Son of the Living God. And not only is He the Son of the Living God, but He commissioned me to preach the Gospel, and I was there . . . .

". . . I was there when we crossed the Sea of Galilee and the storm came. Jesus came walking upon the water! I said, 'If that be You, Lord, bid me come.' I crawled out of the boat, and I walked on the water. And it wasn't until I took my eyes off of Him and started looking at circumstances, Aeneas, that I began to sink. He reached out and grabbed hold of me! We walked back and got into the boat (Matt. 14:28-32).

"After we landed on the other side, I saw this Jesus set free the demoniac of the Gadarenes (Mark 5:1-19). I was walking down the road with Him when the ten lepers came — and they were healed as they went (Luke 17:12-19).

"Aeneas, I was with Jesus when the ruler Jairus came requesting prayer for his daughter. We were on the way to Jairus' house when messengers came and told him, 'Don't bother the

Master any longer; your daughter is dead.' I was there, and I saw it. Jesus turned to Jairus and said, 'Only believe.'

"And, oh, Aeneas, I was there that day in Jairus' house when Jesus took the damsel by the hand and raised her from the dead (Mark 5:35-43)!

"Aeneas, let me tell you something else about Jesus. We were walking down the road one day and saw a funeral procession in Nain. And Jesus went over and raised the young man from the dead (Luke 7:11-15)!

"And, Aeneas, let me tell you something *else*: *Jesus Christ now cures you! Arise and walk!*"

Aeneas' faith was so high that he leaped out of that bed. Jesus Christ, the Man he believed in, had healed him too! And the Word of God says that all of Lydda and Saron saw his healing and turned to the Lord.

Notice that the miracle of his healing occurred *after* the Day of Pentecost. That puts it within this present dispensation of the Holy Spirit, for we are living in the same dispensation as the Early Church. If I have studied the Word of God correctly, then it is true that as long as we are living in the same dispensation, all of the spiritual and scriptural laws pertaining to that dispensation are still in effect. Therefore, healing is still in effect for us today.

Realize the impact of the words Peter spoke to Aeneas: *"Jesus Christ cures you!"*

Since Jesus Christ cures people, and since we are living in the same dispensation, then what right do we have to allow sickness in our bodies? If Jesus Christ has healed us, what right do we have to be even *half* sick?

The Word of God says, *". . . with his stripes we ARE healed"* (Isa. 53:5). Since Jesus Christ has cured us by His stripes, we have no right *not* to be well! Then why do some people remain sick? Why doesn't everyone get healed? The answer can be found in Luke chapter 4.

We read here that Jesus Christ has been traveling throughout Galilee, preaching, teaching, and healing all who were oppressed of the devil. The Bible says that He became well known throughout the region.

Returning to His hometown of Nazareth, however, He encountered only hostility and unbelief when He visited the synagogue.

Jesus began to read to them from the scroll of Isaiah: *"The Spirit of the Lord is upon me, because he hath anointed me to preach the gospel to the poor; he hath sent me to heal the broken-hearted, to preach deliverance to the captives, and recovering of sight to the blind, to set at liberty them that are bruised, To preach the acceptable year of the Lord"* (Luke 4:18,19).

Then Jesus closed the scroll and sat down. All eyes were fastened on Him. He said, *". . . This day is this scripture fulfilled in your ears"* (v. 21).

Oh, what a revival they could have had that day in Nazareth! There was no need for anyone in Nazareth to let the sun set that day on their sin, sickness, disease, or anything else. There was no need for anyone to go to bed that night with any pain left in his or her body. Jesus had just told them that He had come to set them free!

What a celebration they could have had! Why didn't they

receive their healing? It is very simple: They refused to believe. The people said, "The works You did in Capernaum, do here." They said, "Physician, heal Thyself" (Luke 4:23).

I want you to notice something. When Peter said to Aeneas, "Jesus Christ cures you. Arise!" Aeneas arose because Aeneas believed.

If we will only begin to believe what the Word of God says without pulling back from it, we will receive blessing after blessing. It is when we refuse to believe that we do not receive.

Therefore, it is up to you to believe and receive from God. Jesus Christ already has purchased everything for you. It is now up to you to receive it.

God is not going to do anymore about the devil than what

He has done already. It is now up to you to use your authority.

God has done all He is ever going to do about healing you! It is now up to you to receive.

God did all He is ever going to do about healing through Jesus' death, burial, and ressurection. Stripes for our healing were laid upon Jesus one day in a judgement hall in the city of Jerusalem when they took Him down into the lower part of the building.

They stripped the garments from His back, bent Him over, tied Him, and a Roman soldier backed off from Jesus with a whip in his hand. Some say that Roman soldier brought that whip down across the back of Jesus thirty-nine times. Soon His back was cut to ribbons. Blood began to splatter onto the floor. It even began to splatter on that Roman soldier. He didn't even realize that Jesus' blood was being shed for the healing of all sickness and disease.

We talk about Jesus' blood being shed for the redemption of sin. Yes, it was, but that blood also was shed to obtain our healing.

Jesus Christ has healed you. It is now up to you to believe and obey God.

Remember the story of Naaman in Second Kings chapter 5? Naaman was captain of the Syrian army.

The Bible says that a captured Israelite girl was in his household serving as his wife's maid. The little girl said, "I wish my master could go over to Samaria and see the prophet of God. God could heal my master of his leprosy."

Naaman went to Samaria. The prophet Elisha told him, "If you will go dip seven times in the River Jordan, you will be healed." Naaman went and did what the prophet said.

Another Old Testament story tells about the widow of Zarephath (1 Kings 17). That woman took the last morsel of food out of her child's mouth and fed it to the preacher! You see, she and her son had only one meal left before they would starve to death. This preacher named Elijah came by and said, "The Lord said for you to give that food to me."

The widow knew in her heart that he was speaking by the Spirit of God, so she gave him her food. And the Word of God says that because she believed what Elijah said, her household was saved.

These Old Testament principles still apply today: If God said it, we must do it if we are to receive.

The difference between Old and New Testament dispensations is that in the Old Testament, the only ones anointed by the Spirit of God were prophets, priests, and kings.

Today it is not necessary for a prophet to hear from God on our behalf; we can hear the Voice of God ourselves. We have the anointing of the power of God, and we can take what God says in His Word, believe it, act on it, and receive it for ourselves.

That is why it is now up to you to receive whatever you want from God. Everything has been purchased for you. It is now time you arose and received.

Peter said, "Aeneas, Jesus Christ cures you. Arise!"

That same Jesus is still walking up and down the face of the earth by His Holy Spirit — and that same Jesus will cure *you*!

Take that verse of Scripture and put your own name on it: "John, Jesus Christ cures you." "Barbara, Jesus Christ cures you." "Ruth, Jesus Christ cures you." "Ken, Jesus Christ cures you."

I say to you, *"Jesus Christ cures you! Arise and receive your healing — right now!"*

A Sinner's Prayer To Receive Jesus as Savior

Dear Heavenly Father,

I come to You in the Name of Jesus.

Your Word says, "*. . . him that cometh to me I will in no wise cast out*" (John 6:37).

So I know You won't cast me out, but You take me in,

And I thank You for it.

You said in Your Word, "*Whosoever shall call upon the name of the Lord shall be saved*" (Rom. 10:13).

I am calling on Your Name,

So I know You have saved me now.

You also said, "*. . . if thou shalt confess with thy mouth the Lord Jesus, and shalt believe in thine heart that God hath raised him from the dead, thou shalt be saved. For with the heart man*

*believeth unto righteousness; and
with the mouth confession is
made unto salvation"*
(Rom. 10:9,10).

I believe in my heart that Jesus
Christ is the Son of God.

I believe that He was raised from
the dead for my justification.

And I confess Him now as my Lord,

Because Your Word says, "*. . .with
the heart man believeth unto
righteousness. . .*" and I do believe
with my heart,

I have now become the righteousness of God in Christ
(2 Cor. 5:21),

And I am saved!

Thank You, Lord!

Signed _____

Date _____

About the Author

Kenneth Hagin Jr., Executive Vice-President of Kenneth Hagin Ministries and Pastor of RHEMA Bible Church, writes from a rich and diversified background of more than forty years in the ministry.

Rev. Hagin attended Southwestern Assemblies of God College and Oral Roberts University, graduating with a degree in religious education.

After serving as an associate pastor, Rev. Hagin traveled as an evangelist throughout the United states and abroad and was responsible for organizing RHEMA Bible Training Center, a school which equips men and women for the ministry.

In addition to his administrative and teaching responsibilities at RHEMA, Rev. Hagin is senior pastor of RHEMA Bible Church, a large, thriving congregation on the RHEMA campus. He is also International Director of RHEMA Ministerial Association International. Rev. Hagin has a weekly radio program, "RHEMA Radio Church," which is heard on stations throughout the United States, and a television broadcast, "RHEMA Praise."

RHEMA
Bible Training Center

Providing Skilled Laborers for the End-Time Harvest!

Do you desire —

- to find and effectively fulfill God's plan for your life?
- to know how to "rightly divide the Word of truth"?
- to learn how to follow and flow with the Spirit of God?
- to run your God-given race with excellence and integrity?
- to become not only a laborer but a *skilled* laborer?

If so, then RHEMA Bible Training Center is here for you!

For a free video and full-color catalog, call:

1-888-28-FAITH   Offer #602
(1-888-283-2484)

To use our Internet address: http://www.rhema.org

*RHEMA Bible Training Center admits students of
any race, color, or ethnic origin.*

The Word of Faith

The Word of Faith is a full-color monthly magazine with faith-building teaching articles by Rev. Kenneth E. Hagin and Rev. Kenneth Hagin Jr.

The Word of Faith also includes encouraging true-life stories of Christians overcoming circumstances through God's Word, and information on the various outreaches of Kenneth Hagin Ministries and RHEMA Bible Church.

To receive a free subscription to *The Word of Faith*, call:

1-888-28-FAITH   Offer #603
(1-888-283-2484)

To use our Internet address: http://www.rhema.org

RHEMA

ndence Bible School

•Flexible•
Enroll anytime; choose your topic of study;
study at your own pace!

•Affordable•
Pay as you go — only $25 per lesson!
(Price subject to change without notice.)

•Profitable•
"Words cannot adequately describe the
tremendous impact RCBS has had on my life.
I have learned so much, and I am always
sharing my newfound knowledge with everyone I can. I feel like a blind person who has
just had his eyes opened!"

Louisiana

The RHEMA Correspondence Bible
School is a home Bible study course that
can help you in your everyday life!

This course of study has been designed
with the layman in mind, with practical
teaching on prayer, faith, healing, Spirit-
led living, and much more to help you
live a victorious Christian life!

For enrollment information and
course listing call today!

1-888-28-FAITH Offer #604
(1-888-283-2484)

To use our Internet address: http://www.rhema.org

BOOK FAVORITES

ANOTHER LOOK AT FAITH
Kenneth Hagin Jr. • Item #733

This book focuses on what faith is not, thus answering common misunderstandings of what it means to live by faith.

THE BELIEVER'S AUTHORITY
Kenneth E. Hagin • Item #406

This powerful book provides excellent insight into the authority that rightfully belongs to every believer in Christ!

BLESSED IS ... Untying the 'NOTS' That Hinder Your Blessing!
Kenneth Hagin Jr. • Item #736

This book creatively teaches believers from Psalm 1 what *not* to do in order to be blessed by God and receive His richest and best!

DON'T QUIT! Your Faith Will See You Through
Kenneth Hagin Jr. • Item #724

Learn how you can develop faith that won't quit and come out of tests or trials victoriously.

FAITH FOOD DEVOTIONS
Kenneth E. Hagin • Item #045

Rev. Kenneth E. Hagin's beautiful, hardcover devotional book, *Faith Food Devotions*, contains 365 bite-sized teachings and faith-filled confessions for triumphant Christian living every day of the year!

FOLLOWING GOD'S PLAN FOR YOUR LIFE
Kenneth E. Hagin • Item #519

It's up to individual Christians to fulfill the divine purpose that God ordained for their lives before the beginning of time. This book can help believers stay on the course God has set before them!

To order any of these items or for a complete listing
of our Faith Library materials, please call:

1-888-28-FAITH (1-888-283-2484)

Mention #605 when ordering

To use our Internet address: http://www.rhema.org

BOOK FAVORITES

GOD'S WORD: A Never-Failing Remedy
Kenneth E. Hagin • Item #526

The never-failing remedy for every adversity of life can be found in the pages of God's holy written Word! And when you act on the Word, it truly becomes a never-failing remedy!

THE HEALING ANOINTING
Kenneth E. Hagin • Item #527

This dynamic book explores the operation of God's powerful anointing in divine healing.

HEALING: Forever Settled
Kenneth E. Hagin • Item #723

The primary question among believers is whether it's God's will to heal people today. Healing is a forever-settled subject because God's Word is forever settled!

HOW TO LIVE WORRY-FREE
Kenneth Hagin Jr. • Item #735

Sound teaching from God's Word is combined with practical insights to illustrate the perils of worry and to help guide the believer into the peace of God.

HOW YOU CAN BE LED BY THE SPIRIT OF GOD
Kenneth E. Hagin • Item #513

These step-by-step guidelines based on the Scriptures can help Christians avoid spiritual pitfalls and follow the Spirit of God in every area of life.

IT'S YOUR MOVE!
Kenneth Hagin Jr. • Item #730

Move out of the arena of discouragement and despair and into the arena of God's blessings that are yours in Christ.

To order any of these items or for a complete listing of our Faith Library materials, please call:

1-888-28-FAITH (1-888-283-2484)

Mention #605 when ordering

To use our Internet address: http://www.rhema.org

BOOK FAVORITES

JESUS — NAME ABOVE ALL NAMES
Kenneth Hagin Jr. • Item #737

This exciting book discusses the redemptive realities and blessings that every believer inherits at salvation through the power of Jesus' Name.

LOVE: The Way Victory
Kenneth E. Hagin • Item #523

By acting on the truths contained in this book, believers can turn around seemingly impossible situations in their lives — just by walking in the God-kind of love!

THE TRIUMPHANT CHURCH:
Dominion Over All the Powers of Darkness
Kenneth E. Hagin • Item #520

This bestseller is a comprehensive biblical study of the origin and operation of Satan that shows believers how to enforce his defeat in their lives.

THE UNTAPPED POWER IN PRAISE
Kenneth Hagin Jr. • Item #725

The power of God is available to set believers free. This book teaches how to tap into that power through praise!

WELCOME TO GOD'S FAMILY:
A Foundational Guide for Spirit-Filled Living
Kenneth E. Hagin • Item #528

Increase your spiritual effectiveness by discovering what it means to be born again and how you can partake of the biblical benefits that God has provided for you as His child!

To order any of these items or for a complete listing of our Faith Library materials, please call:

1-888-28-FAITH (1-888-283-2484)

Mention #605 when ordering

To use our Internet address: http://www.rhema.org

FAITH LIBRARY PUBLICATIONS

AUDIOTAPE FAVORITES

ANSWERED PRAYER: An Obtainable Goal Series
Kenneth E. Hagin • Item #50H • 4-Tape Series

When a believer prays in line with God's Word, his prayers will always be effective. This series presents scriptural steps that, when followed faithfully, can assure an answer to prayer.

FAITH CLASSICS
Kenneth E. Hagin • Item #16H • 6-Tape Series

These all-time bestselling messages on the fundamentals of faith continue to change the lives of countless believers!

HOW TO BE AN OVERCOMER
Kenneth E. Hagin Jr. • Item #21J • 4-Tape Series

As a believer, you already possess all the spiritual tools you need to put you over in life. This series shows how to exercise your authority in Christ and take possession of what rightfully belongs to you!

MINISTERING TO THE LORD
Kenneth E. Hagin • Item #33H • 4-Tape Series

This special series shares scriptural truths and personal insight on praise and worship.

SOARING WITH THE EAGLES SERIES
Kenneth E. Hagin Jr. • Item #35J • 2-Tape Series

This series inspires believers to focus on God and receive the supernatural strength needed to soar above life's storms.

VICTORY: God's Plan For You
Kenneth E. Hagin Jr. • Item #29J • 3-Tape Series

Believers can boldly face tests and trials because God has drawn a master plan for them — a plan that always spells victory!

To order any of these items or for a complete listing
of our Faith Library materials, please call:

1-888-28-FAITH (1-888-283-2484)

Mention #611 when ordering

To use our Internet address: http://www.rhema.org

VIDEOTAPE FAVORITES

BORN TO RAZE HELL!
Kenneth E. Hagin • Item #VCH10

This video vividly explains how Jesus Christ empowers believers to destroy the works of the devil in their lives!

EL SHADDAI: The God Who Is More Than Enough
Kenneth E. Hagin • Item #VCH09

In this classic video, Rev. Kenneth E. Hagin boldly proclaims what God will do for those who set their love upon Him!

IS YOUR HOUSE REALLY A HOME SERIES
Kenneth Hagin Jr. • Item #VSJ1 • 4-Volume Series

You can turn your house into a loving home by listening to and applying the biblical principles in this dynamic teaching series on the home and family.

THE BELIEVER'S AUTHORITY SERIES
Kenneth E. Hagin • Item #VSH1 • 3-Volume Series

Based on the Book of Ephesians, this exciting videotape series provides an in-depth study of the believer's authority in Christ.

WHAT TO DO WHEN FAITH SEEMS WEAK AND VICTORY LOST SERIES
Kenneth E. Hagin • Item #VSH2 • 2-Volume Series

Discover some vital steps you can take to turn seemingly hopeless situations into occasions of victory and rejoicing!

WHEN THE SPIRIT GETS TO MOVIN'
Kenneth E. Hagin • Item #VCH11

Witness and share in the powerful move of God that occurred during this extraordinary meeting as captured on videotape.

To order any of these items or for a complete listing
of our Faith Library materials, please call:

1-888-28-FAITH (1-888-283-2484)

Mention #612 when ordering

To use our Internet address: http://www.rhema.org

MINISTRY RESOURCES

A YEAR AT THE LORD'S TABLE
RHEMA Bible Church Pastoral Staff • Item #SRB6

This manual includes a sermon outline for each of its twelve audiotaped messages taught by the RHEMA Bible Church pastoral staff to celebrate the redemptive work of Christ through the Communion service.

THE MINISTRY OF HELPS
Item #955

This quick-reference guide covers many of the major aspects of the ministry of helps. Subjects include: Developing Prayer Groups in the Church, The Church Music Program, and 14 other pertinent topics!

MISSIONARY STRATEGIES
Item #957

Believers called to the mission field will find this book a tremendous aid in preparing to pursue God's call. *Missionary Strategies* will also help those who have a heart for missions to better understand and respond to a missionary's unique needs.

THE PASTORAL MINISTRY
Item #954

This comprehensive manual contains practical information regarding issues that relate to churches. Topics include: Effective Pastoring, Church Insurance Needs, Church Legalities, and many more.

PIONEERING STRATEGIES
Item #956

This book was written by ordained RHEMA Ministerial Association International pastors who have successfully pioneered churches. *Pioneering Strategies* gives ministers practical business information, inspiration, and encouragement to help them establish a new work!

To order any of these items or for a complete listing
of our Faith Library materials, please call:

1-888-28-FAITH (1-888-283-2484)

Mention #614 when ordering

To use our Internet address: http://www.rhema.org

MUSIC FAVORITES

HE'LL DO IT AGAIN!
RHEMA Singers & Band
Cassette: MS07-C • Compact Disc: MS07-CD

INSTRUMENTAL PRAISE
RHEMA Singers & Band
Cassette: MS09-C • Compact Disc: MS09-CD

LOOK WHAT THE LORD HAS DONE!
RHEMA Singers & Band
Cassette: MS10-C • Compact Disc: MS10-CD

THE REASON FOR IT ALL (Christmas)
RHEMA Singers & Band
Cassette: MS08-C • Compact Disc: MS08-CD

TRUST AND OBEY
Joel Siegel
Cassette: MS11-C • Compact Disc: MS11-CD

RHEMA Singers & Band (RS&B) has developed 22 accompaniment trax for your singing pleasure Call for listings.

To order any of these items or for a complete listing
of our Faith Library materials, please call:

1-888-28-FAITH (1-888-283-2484)
Mention #613 when ordering
To use our Internet address: http://www.rhema.org